ENORMOUS
BOOBS

First published 1998.
Reprinted 1999 (twice).

Summersdale Publishers Ltd
46 West Street
Chichester
West Sussex
PO19 1RP
United Kingdom

ISBN 1 84024 042 3

Printed and bound in Great Britain.

www.summersdale.com

ENORMOUS BOOBS

The Greatest Mistakes in the History of the World

Stewart Ferris

SUMMERSDALE

'We all know that a leopard
cannot change his stripes.'
            Vice President Al Gore

Contents

Introduction

'The man who does things makes many mistakes, but he never makes the biggest mistake of all – doing nothing.'

Benjamin Franklin

Boobs – small, medium and enormous – litter human history like fast food packaging. This book doesn't set out to apportion blame for this, although it would probably help if they put more bins out. Besides, it's human nature to make mistakes: the first identifiable enormous boob was our ancestors' decision to come down from the trees. As you will read, things have gone pretty well downhill ever since.

Marketing
Boobs

An American baby food manufacturer decided to export its products to Africa, using the same cute baby on the label that they used at home. When sales were not what they expected, they found out why . . . in Africa companies only put pictures on the label of what is actually inside the tin, since most people could not read.

ENORMOUS BOOBS

The Los Angeles Times unwittingly juxtaposed an ad banner demanding that readers 'Follow that Fool!' above a photo.

The photo was of a sombre Zairian man being marched to his death by rebel soldiers just moments before execution.

The Beatles were turned down by a number of record companies before they finally secured a deal. A representative from one of them explained his reasoning: he believed guitar-based groups were on their way out.

The first canned food was sold in 1812. The first can-opener, however, didn't appear until 1860.

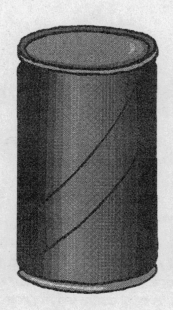

Criminal and Legal Boobs

An American man thought his insurance company boobed when they agreed to insure his box of rare and expensive cigars against fire. He then smoked all of the cigars within a month, and filed a claim against the insurance company stating that he had lost them in a series of small fires. The insurance company refused to pay out, claiming that he had consumed the cigars in the normal fashion. He went on to sue them, and won his case. He was able to win the case because the insurance company had agreed that the cigars were insurable against fire, and had not defined what was an 'acceptable' form of fire. Rather than bothering to appeal, which would have been costly for the insurance company, it agreed to pay the man $15,000 to compensate for the loss of the cigars. However, the insurance company then had the man arrested on 24 counts of arson, and was able to use his own insurance claim and testimony from the previous case as evidence against him. They won the case, and the man was sentenced to 24 consecutive one-year prison terms.

When a Washington man tried to commit a robbery, there were several indications that this was his first (and last) offence. The shop he tried to rob happened to be a gun shop, and it was also full of customers, many of whom carried their own guns. There was a police car parked outside, and a uniformed officer was inside, standing next to the counter. The robber saw the police officer and announced a hold-up, firing some shots into the ceiling. The officer and the shopkeeper both returned fire, killing him. Several other customers also drew their weapons, but didn't fire.

A young thief boobed when he tried to steal a handbag from an old lady who was sitting inside a photo booth waiting for the machine to take her picture. Not only did he flee empty-handed having failed to wrench the bag from her grip, but he also appeared very clearly in one of her photos, for which the police were very grateful. He was arrested the next day.

ENORMOUS BOOBS

A young pregnant woman became unnerved when a fellow bus passenger stared at her, smiling. She changed her seat, but he became even more amused. She moved again and then on her fourth move he burst out laughing. She had him arrested and the case came to court. His explanation of his behaviour was,

"When the lady boarded the bus I couldn't help noticing she was pregnant. She sat under an advertisement which read 'Coming Soon The Gold Dust Twins'; then she moved under one that read 'Sloans Liniments remove Swelling'. I was even more amused when she sat under a shaving advertisement which read 'William Stick Did The Trick'. Then I could not control myself any longer when

on the fourth move she sat under an advertisement which read 'Dunlop Rubber would have prevented this accident'."
He won the case.

Gloucester town council passed a housing law making it illegal for tenants in public housing to die without giving at least 30 days notice.

In the Middle Ages, there was a law in England which stated that any condemned man who could withdraw his head from the Gibbet (a forerunner to the guillotine) in between the time when the blade was released to when it hit the bottom, and then run to a nearby town, could be pardoned. One man achieved this feat, and took great pleasure in boasting about it for years afterwards. His story became so tiresome that people started to think he had made it up. The man therefore decided to prove his story by putting his neck under the Gibbet again. This time, of course, the blade cut his head off.

An American woman was arrested in Texas after a mechanic reported to police that 18 packages of marijuana were packed in the engine compartment of her car which she had brought to the mechanic for an oil change. Apparently, she didn't realise that the mechanic would have to raise the bonnet to change the oil.

A woman was arrested in Florida for attempting to rob a motel. She was armed with only an electric chainsaw, which was not plugged in.

CRIMINAL AND LEGAL BOOBS

A man walked into a Burger King in Michigan at 7:50am, flashed a gun and demanded cash. The server turned him down because he said he couldn't open the till without a food order. When the man ordered onion rings, the server said they weren't available for breakfast. The man, frustrated, walked away.

A Belgian man suspected of robbing a jewellery store in Liege said he couldn't have done it. His iron-clad alibi was that, 'I was busy breaking into a school at the same time'. Police then arrested him for breaking into the school.

During a trial for possession of drugs, the defence claimed that their client had been searched without a warrant. The prosecutor pointed out that a warrant wasn't necessary when a suspect had a bulge in their jacket that might have been a gun. The defendent happened to be wearing the same jacket in court that day, and handed it over to the judge so that he could see for himself that it wasn't a gun. The judge looked in the inside pocket and found a bulbous packet of cocaine. Unable to control his laughter, he had to call a recess.

In Alabama, a man was injured after he attempted to replace a fuse in his car with a rifle bullet which happened to be a perfect fit. Of course, when electricity heated the bullet, it went off and shot him in the knee.

ENORMOUS BOOBS

When two robbers tried to pull the front off a cash machine, they attached a chain from the machine to the bumper of their car. Instead of pulling the front panel off the machine, though, they pulled the bumper off their car. They became nervous and quickly drove off, leaving the chain still attached to the machine, with the bumper still attached to the chain, and with the car's number plate attached to the bumper.

A man walked into a police station and dropped a bag of cocaine on the counter. He informed the desk sergeant that it was sub-standard cut, and asked that the person who sold it to him be arrested immediately.

ENORMOUS BOOBS

A robber walked into a shop and demanded all the money in the till. The shopkeeper handed him the money, and the robber left . . . leaving his wallet on the counter.

English customs officials chatted about golf to a German man who was entering the country carrying a large golf bag. The man claimed to be on a golfing holiday, but it soon became clear to the customs officials that he didn't know what a golf handicap was. The man was then asked to demonstrate his swing, which he duly performed backwards. The contents of his bag were then inspected and a large quantity of drugs was discovered.

A German woman seeking the ultimate in skin lotion decided that she would bathe in the milk of a camel. So she stole a camel from the local zoo and transported it back to her house, where she realised that the camel's name was 'Otto'.

A company called 'Guns For Hire' that specialised in staging gunfights for Western movies, etc received a call from a woman who wanted to have her husband killed. She got a life sentence.

ENORMOUS BOOBS

When a convicted robber negotiated a deal to pay compensation in lieu of serving a few months in prison, he paid the court with a forged cheque. They sentenced him to 10 years.

A robber burst into a shop brandishing a gun and announced a hold-up. Before anyone could get a good look at his face, however, he pulled a bag over his head . . . and then realised he had forgotten to put any eye holes in the bag.

An American burglar broke into a bank late one night and stole the bank's security camera. The camera was recording onto a tape in another part of the building, leaving police a full and clear video recording of the man's face as he stole the camera.

Another bank robber broke into a bank's basement through a street-level window, cutting himself up pretty badly in the process. He then realised that he had no access to any of the bank's money from where he was, and that he couldn't climb back outside through the same window. He was bleeding so much from his injuries that he had to phone the emergency services to rescue him.

An American robber walked into a shop, put a $20 bill on the counter, and asked for change. When the shopkeeper opened the till, the robber pulled a gun and asked for all the cash in the till, which the shopkeeper promptly provided. The man took the cash and fled – leaving the $20 bill on the counter. The total amount of cash he had got from the drawer was just $15.

A man was arrested at a US airport hotel after he tried to pass two (counterfeit) $16 bills.

ENORMOUS BOOBS

A thief in Salisbury boobed when he tried to get a suntan. He stole some doctors' paging devices from a hospital store room, then while making his escape, he spotted a vertical sunbed. He undressed, and switched on the machine, standing there for 45 minutes. The machine has a maximum dosage of 10 seconds, however. Having exceeded this by almost 300 times, he was covered in painful blisters and ended up scarred for life.

A criminal suspect was interrogated by mischievous police by placing a metal colander on his head and connecting it with wires to a photocopier. The message 'He's lying' was placed in the photocopier, and the police pressed the copy button each time they thought the suspect wasn't telling the truth. Believing the 'Lie Detector' was working, the suspect confessed.

ENORMOUS BOOBS

A City Council in California enacted a ban on nuclear weapons, and set a $500 fine for anyone who detonated one within city limits.

When two petrol station attendants refused to hand over their takings to a drunk and rather dim robber, the man threatened to call the police. They still refused, so the robber called the police and was arrested.

ENORMOUS BOOBS

A terrorist made an enormous boob when he sent a letter bomb but failed to put sufficient postage on it. The bomb was delivered back to him marked 'return to sender' . . . he opened it and survived the blast, albeit without his face.

The electric chair was introduced as a form of execution in the United States at the end of the nineteenth century. The concept so impressed the emperor of Ethiopia at the time that he ordered three of them.

When he realised that they would not work without electricity (which was yet to be introduced to his country) he used one of them as his throne.

ENORMOUS BOOBS

A Los Angeles man who later said he was 'tired of walking', stole a steamroller and led police on a 5 mph chase until an officer stepped aboard and brought the vehicle to a stop.

A New York man was arrested by police for disorderly conduct after he frightened a bank teller by handing in a note that read, 'Don't be alarmed – this is a bank deposit – please take the money out of the envelope and deposit it into my account'.

ENORMOUS BOOBS

A man boobed when attempting to rob a diving shop to raise enough money to buy diving lessons for his wife. Having ransacked the till in the middle of the night, he spotted an old brass diving helmet in the shop and couldn't resist trying it on. The helmet got stuck, so he decided to make his escape with it still on his head. He stepped outside into the road and was run over by lorry.

A stupid criminal held up a 24-hour store with a starter's gun which could only fire blanks. The shopkeeper managed to wrestle the gun from the criminal's hands, and then pointed the gun at the criminal until the police arrived. During this time, the criminal made no attempt to escape and repeatedly begged 'please don't shoot!'.

Transport Boobs

A Frenchwoman was killed when her car crashed into a tree near Marseilles. She had been distracted from the road by the beeping of her pet Tamagotchi, attached to her key ring. Rather than let the little cyber pet die, she tried to save it and thus killed herself.

In Australia, the driver of a large articulated lorry noticed something wrong with his brakes as he drove through the desert, so he stopped to check them out. Instead of smoking brakes he found a mangled Porsche stuck to his front bumper, inside which was an extremely irate driver. The driver of the Porsche had earlier tried to overtake the lorry, but the road had narrowed very suddenly and when he cut in front of the lorry the two vehicles clipped each other, causing the Porsche to turn sideways and become wedged on the front of the lorry. As far as the lorry driver was concerned, he simply thought he had run over a pothole when the accident happened.

An Australian died while train surfing. Although he was on a diesel train, the track merged with one used by electric trains. This track had overhead power cables, into which he slammed at considerable speed. Little trace was left of him.

A police officer from the Arizona Highway Patrol discovered a smouldering pile of metal embedded into the side of a cliff rising above the road at the apex of a curve. It looked as if an aeroplane had crashed into the side of the cliff, but actually it was a car.

The driver had somehow obtained a JATO (Jet Assisted Take Off) unit, a kind of solid fuel rocket used to give heavy transport planes extra speed when taking off from short runways. He had taken his car out into the desert, found a long, straight stretch of road, affixed the rocket to the back of his car, and ignited it. Ignition must have occurred 3 miles from the crash site, according to the scorched and melted road. The rocket would have accelerated to full speed within 5 seconds, pushing the car to over 350 mph, and continued at full power for a further 20 seconds. The car remained on the road for a couple of miles before the driver attempted to brake. This resulted in the brakes completely melting and the tyres exploding. He then became airborne for the final mile of his life, impacting the cliff face at a height of 125 feet and leaving a 3 feet deep crater in the rock. The only parts of the driver that were found were fragments of bone, fingernails, teeth and hair.

ENORMOUS BOOBS

In England, a foolish man died attempting to demonstrate his theory that railway power cables did not contain any current while the train was stationary.

A drunken man was walking along a railway track on his way home when he fell over and passed out with his left arm and his left leg lying on the track. A train came along and severed them both. This would seem to be unfortunate enough for anyone, but almost exactly ten years later the same man fell drunkenly onto a railway track again and managed to lose his other arm and leg!

ENORMOUS BOOBS

Three Brazilians were flying at low altitude in a plane when another plane flew close by. They decided it would be fun to 'drop a moonie' at the other plane, but in doing so they lost control of the plane and crashed. The three bodies were found inside the aircraft with their pants around their ankles.

Translation
Boobs

ENORMOUS BOOBS

A chicken company's slogan, 'It takes a tough man to make a tender chicken,' was translated into Spanish as, 'It takes a sexually stimulated man to make a chicken affectionate.' The company's owner was pictured next to one of his chicken with this slogan on billboards all over Mexico.

When Vicks first introduced its cough drops on the German market, they were disappointed to learn that the German pronunciation of 'v' is 'f' – which in German is the slang for sexual penetration.

ENORMOUS BOOBS

The Vauxhall Nova was not well suited to Spanish speaking countries. 'No Va' means 'It Does Not Go' in Spanish.

Ford had a similar translation problem in Brazil when its 'Pinto' flopped. It turned out that Pinto was Brazilian slang for 'small male genitalia'. Ford re-badged all the cars as 'Corcel', which means horse.

ENORMOUS BOOBS

When Pepsi first exported to Taiwan, their slogan was 'Come alive with the Pepsi Generation'. This was translated into Chinese rather too literally as 'Pepsi Brings Your Ancestors Back from the Grave.'

*C*oca-Cola had a similar problem. Their first exports to China were given a name that when pronounced sounded like 'Coca-Cola' - Ke-kou-ke-la. Unfortunately, the characters used meant 'Bite The Wax Tadpole' (or 'female horse stuffed with wax' depending on the dialect), but thousands of signs had been printed before this was realised. A close phonetic equivalent, 'ko-kou-ko-le', was eventually found that translated more favourably as 'Happiness In The Mouth'.

ENORMOUS BOOBS

Also in Chinese, the Kentucky Fried Chicken slogan 'finger-lickin' good' came out as 'eat your fingers off.'

When Clairol introduced a curling iron, known as 'Mist Stick', into Germany, they found out that mist is slang for manure. Manure sticks were not too popular.

ENORMOUS BOOBS

When Parker marketed a ball-point pen in Mexico, its ads were intended to say 'It won't leak in your pocket and embarrass you'. However, the company mistakenly thought the Spanish word 'embarazar' meant embarrass. Instead the ads stated that 'It won't leak in your pocket and make you pregnant'.

An American clothing manufacturer printed T-shirts for the Spanish market which promoted a visit by the Pope. Instead of their shirts saying 'I Saw the Pope' in Spanish, they actually said 'I Saw the Potato'.

ENORMOUS BOOBS

When a range of products called 'Big John' were launched in French-speaking parts of Canada, they were re-named as 'Gros Jos' until the manufacturers found out that the phrase, in slang, means 'big breasts'.

An Italian campaign for Schweppes Tonic Water translated the name as 'Schweppes Toilet Water'.

ENORMOUS BOOBS

Scandinavian vacuum manufacturer Electrolux used the following in an American ad campaign: 'Nothing sucks like an Electrolux.'

Colgate introduced a toothpaste in France called 'Cue', which shared the name of a French pornographic magazine.

TRANSLATION BOOBS

ENORMOUS BOOBS

All airline pilots are supposed to speak English when communicating by radio. But recently, a Chinese pilot of a Boeing 737 airliner was heard to say 'What does "pull up" mean?' while trying to make an instrument landing in dark, rainy conditions. It was the flight deck's computer, telling him in English to pull up. The aircraft ploughed into a hill.

Animal
Boobs

When two Italian sailors arrived in Australia to compete for the America's Cup in 1986, they went out for a day to see a bit of bush country. A kangaroo jumped in front of their hire car and they couldn't avoid hitting him. They were shocked, thinking they had killed it, but not so shocked that they couldn't have some fun. One of them propped the carcass up against their vehicle, while the other dressed it up in an expensive Gucci blazer and took a photo. The kangaroo, which had merely been stunned, suddenly took off into the bush taking with it the Gucci blazer plus the cash and passport contained in its pocket.

In Cairo, 6 people drowned in an attempt to save a chicken that had fallen down a well. An 18 year old farmer was the first to descend into the well, but he drowned when an undercurrent of water pulled him down. Then his sister and two brothers came down the well, one at a time, to save him. All three drowned. Finally, two elderly farmers tried to help, but they two were pulled down by the same undercurrent. The bodies of the six people were later pulled out of the well by police. The chicken was also pulled out, alive.

Whilst driving home one night, a man ran over a cat that was crossing the road. He pulled in and stepped outside to look for the cat, and found it lying at the side of the road. The impact had been quite hard, and he thought it kindest to put the moggy out of its misery. He took the steering lock from the car and clubbed the cat repeatedly on the head with it. Satisfied that the cat was truly dead, he continued his journey home.

Later that night, some police officers knocked at his door investigating a report of animal cruelty. He told them what he had done, and the policemen checked the front of his car to verify the story. Embedded in the radiator grill they found the remains of the cat he had run over. The cat he had clubbed to death was, in fact, a perfectly healthy beast belonging to an elderly neighbour. Apparently, this cat used to enjoy sleeping by the side of the road.

Two animal rights protesters were killed outside a slaughterhouse in Germany by the very pigs they had set free. The two thousand pigs stampeded, trampling them to death.

A German zookeeper fed his constipated elephant a large dose of laxative, plus some prunes, berries and figs in order to help clear the blockage. When finally the animal released its load the force of the expulsion knocked the hapless zookeeper over and suffocated him under a mound of dung.

An American man bought a new four wheel drive jeep and went duck hunting with a friend and his dog. They drove to a frozen lake and set about trying to clear a hole in the ice so that they could float their decoys. The best way to clear a hole big enough for passing ducks to land in was to use dynamite, so they lit a stick with a 40 second fuse and threw it as far as they could onto the frozen lake. The trusty dog did what any dog would do at that point, and ran off to retrieve the stick of dynamite. Nothing the two men did could dissuade the dog from this course of action, and it picked up the dynamite in its mouth and began to run back to its masters, tail wagging. By now the men were getting hysterical, shouting and waving their arms at the dog to drop the dynamite, all of which simply encouraged it. In desperation, one of the men picked up his shotgun and shot the dog. But being full of duck shot, the blast wasn't sufficient to kill the dog, merely making it pause in confusion. So the man fired again, this time really frightening the dog and causing it to seek cover . . . underneath the brand new four wheel drive jeep. After a couple of seconds, the dog and the jeep exploded and sunk into the lake.

The cost of cleaning up and rehabilitating seals after the Exxon Valdez oil spill in Alaska was in the region $80,000 per animal. A special ceremony was held to release publicly back into the wild two of the most expensively saved animals. Unfortunately, just a minute later they were both eaten by a killer whale.

Deadly
Boobs

A n enormous boob occurred in a South African hospital. An observant nurse noticed that many of their dying patients had one thing in common: they had all stayed in the same room in intensive care. Doctors monitored the situation, and noticed that two more patients died unexpectedly in that room. A team was brought in to investigate possible causes, and many precautionary measures were taken: the room was fumigated; the air conditioning unit was checked; all medical equipment was thoroughly serviced; and all the furniture was replaced in case a rare virus was nestled in it. But in spite of all this, the very next patient in the room died during the night. Doctors now suspected criminal involvement of some kind, and decided to monitor the room even more closely. What they discovered late that night was that a cleaner came into the ward every night with an electric floor polishing machine. There was only one plug socket in this ward, however, and she therefore unplugged the life support system each night in order to provide power for her polisher, completely oblivious to the consequences.

A riveter working on a ship in the early twentieth century was ensuring a watertight seal on the ship's outer hull by working in the narrow cavity between the outer hull and the inner hull. Having got his rivets in place perfectly, he realised to his horror that he had sealed himself in between the two layers of steel. The ship was completed by his mystified colleagues, and served many years of active service. When finally the ship was scrapped, workmen dismantling it found a skeleton and some riveting tools between the two hulls.

A man shot himself while using his gun as a club to smash someone's windscreen. It went off and shot him in the abdomen, killing him.

A 47 year old man accidentally killed himself by attempting to answer a telephone. The phone was ringing by the side of his bed, but when he reached for it he picked up his revolver instead. When he put it to his ear, he shot himself.

A man was charged with murder for the death of his cousin. The two of them had decided to play a game of Russian roulette using a semi-automatic pistol. Traditionally, this game is played using a revolver in which all the bullet chambers are empty except for one, giving the player reasonable odds of surviving. A semi-automatic weapon, however, will always fire even if there is only one bullet. One cousin aimed the gun at his cousin's head and fired.

DEADLY BOOBS

ENORMOUS BOOBS

A soldier was crushed to death in his barrack room when he tied a hammock between two wall lockers. When he lay in the hammock, the lockers were pulled in on him, killing him.

A couple of Taiwanese tourists on safari in South Africa's Kruger Park were bitterly disappointed that the lions they found were doing nothing more entertaining than sleeping in the shade. In his quest for some exciting photos, one of them walked over to the sleeping lions, tried to agitate them by nudging them with his foot and shouting, and then started to walk back to the vehicle. Unsurprisingly, he didn't make it.

DEADLY BOOBS

ENORMOUS BOOBS

A group of rather eccentric gentleman had been drinking together when one of them suggested they strip off and play some 'men's games'. The games began with them hitting each other on the head with frozen turnips, but things became more serious when one of the men grabbed a chainsaw and cut off part of his foot. Impressed by this, another man grabbed the chainsaw shouting 'Watch this, then!' and took a swing at his neck, cutting his head off. One of the other men later said, 'It's funny, because when he was young he put on his sister's underwear. But he died like a man.'

More than 60 years ago, a Hollywood actress called Lupe Velez tried to kill herself by overdosing on sleeping pills. She didn't take enough, however, and rushed for the bathroom feeling violently sick. As she entered the bathroom she slipped on the tiled floor and fell head first into the toilet where she drowned.

DEADLY BOOBS

ENORMOUS BOOBS

A French scuba diver unintentionally boobed by being in the wrong place at the wrong time. What started out as a pleasant afternoon swimming amongst fish on a hot summer day end up with him being scooped from the water by a helicopter carried a few miles inland, and dropped into the middle of a raging forest fire where he burnt to death wedged half way up a tree.

A man killed himself with a combination of a terrible diet and no ventilation. A post mortem showed large amounts of methane gas in his system, and it turned out that his diet consisted of large amounts of beans and cabbage. He died in his sleep from breathing in the poisonous gas in his virtually airtight bedroom. Three of his rescue workers became sick, and one was hospitalised.

An unfortunate Yorkshireman dropped his car keys down a drain after he had spent an evening in a remote pub, drinking. He could see them glinting on some dry leaves inside the drain, so he lifted it up and leaned in. The keys were just a little too far for his arms, so he leaned in further and promptly fell in, head first. Although he was stuck, he was uninjured and managed to cry for help for several hours. No one heard him, however, and when it began to rain in the middle of the night the drain quickly filled with water and he drowned.

An unhappy Frenchman boobed somewhat whilst trying to kill himself. He stood at the top of a high cliff, tied a noose around his head and secured the other end to a wooden stake. To make sure nothing was left to chance, he then drank some poison and set fire to himself. As if this wasn't enough, he even tried to shoot himself in the head. But he was a poor shot . . . the bullet missed him, and instead cut the rope in half. He fell into the sea, where the water put out the fire and the sudden cold made him vomit up his poison. He was rescued from the sea, but later died in hospital from the exposure.

Not-so-
Deadly
Boobs

A psychology student rented out her spare room to a man in order to nag him constantly and study his reactions. After weeks of being nagged, he finally snapped and beat her repeatedly with an axe. She was left mentally retarded.

A woman, entering her kitchen, was horrified to see her husband shaking violently with what looked like a wire running from his body towards the electric kettle. Thinking he was being electrocuted, she attempted to jolt him away from the source of the current by hitting him hard with a plank of wood from the garden. The impact fractured his arm in two places, which annoyed him greatly as he had only been listening to a personal stereo.

A man entered a hospital after an unusual kind of overdose: he had just returned from a Cuban holiday during which he spent most of his time in brothels and had been introduced to erectile cream for the first time. Although instructed to use it sparingly, he used far more than the recommended amount because he was having so much fun. He now complained to the doctors of a permanent erection: his penile tissue and testicles were painfully swollen, and all the doctors could do was to prescribe painkillers. They assured him that his penis would return to flaccidity within a few days, but they also told him to make the most of his erection as it would be his last.

ENORMOUS BOOBS

A pair of boobs caused a string of strange accidents: a woman received a head wound from falling masonry, a man received whiplash injuries, another man suffered torn gums, and a second woman had two fingers bitten off. What had happened was that the first woman had flashed her breasts at her husband as he left for work. A passing taxi driver saw this, and crashed into the corner of an adjacent medical building. Inside this building, a dental technician was cleaning the second man's teeth when the noise of the crash made her jump, causing her to tear the man's gums with a cleaning pick. In shock, the man instinctively bit off two of her fingers. The woman who had flashed her boobs was then struck by a piece of the medical building falling onto her head.

An eccentric man was admitted to hospital with a shotgun wound to his leg. The reason for his predicament, he explained, was that he had seen a spider crawling up his leg, so he shot it.

ENORMOUS BOOBS

A barmy commuter in Tokyo caused chaos on a crowded tube train one morning when his rubber underpants unexpectedly inflated to 30 times their original size. He had designed them himself as an automatic means of protection from drowning in the event of a tidal wave, but when they went off on the train they began to suffocate his fellow commuters. They were only saved by the quick thinking of one passenger who managed to burst the underpants with a pencil.

A group of drunken men were walking across a high bridge in the early hours of the morning when one of them mentioned that a friend of his had bungee jumped from the bridge. With inebriated enthusiasm, the men decided to have a go themselves. Unfortunately, none had brought any bungee rope with them. Not to be discouraged, one of them suggested using a coil of cable that lay nearby. One end of the cable was duly tied around his leg, and the other was secured to the bridge. He bravely dived off the side of the bridge, plunging 40 feet until the cable tightened and pulled his foot off at the ankle. He survived the fall into the icy waters below, but his foot was never recovered.

High Rise
Boobs

An electrician was working up a telegraph pole when he began to be annoyed by an uncomfortable stone in his shoe. Removing the shoe from his elevated position would have been impossible, so he shook his foot in an effort to reposition the stone. Unfortunately, a well-meaning passer-by noticed the man shaking at the top of the telegraph pole and naturally assumed he was being electrocuted. Trying to save the electrician's life, the passer-by pushed the ladder out from underneath him, causing him to fall to the ground. The electrician broke both legs and compacted three vertebrae.

A 39 year old lawyer died while demonstrating the safety of the windows in a Toronto skyscraper. He crashed through the glass and fell 24 floors to his death.

When working up on a sloping roof it makes sense to tie yourself to something secure, such as a chimney, in case you slip. An American man did just this, except that as he had no chimney he chose to tie the rope to his car which was parked on the other side of the house. He tied the knots meticulously, one around the car's nudge bar and the other around his waist, and made sure there was enough slack to allow him to work without being able to fall very far should he slip. The only aspect in which he boobed was in neglecting to tell his wife . . . she got into the car and drove off. Fortunately she noticed something was dragging behind her, and he was not seriously injured.

An amateur radio operator made an enormous boob while building himself an 80 foot radio transmitter mast. He was using a large quantity of heavy tools and equipment in order to complete the top of the mast, and when he had finished it seemed like a good idea to lower the items to the ground using a pulley. He climbed down, secured a rope at ground level, then climbed back up to load the tools into a barrel. He then climbed down once again and untied the rope, holding on tightly with the intention of letting the barrel fall slowly under his control. Unfortunately, he had miscalculated the weight of the tools in the barrel . . . they weighed almost twice as much as he did! So surprised was he at being yanked upwards by the weight of the falling barrel that he forgot to let go of the rope. Half way up the tower, he crashed into the barrel coming down, fracturing his skull and collarbone. He didn't stop, though, and continued rising until his knuckles hit the pulley. Despite the pain, he managed to hold onto the rope. When the barrel hit the ground, the bottom fell out of it, releasing all its contents. Suddenly he weighed a great deal more than the barrel, and began rapidly to fall. Half way down, he met the barrel coming up, fracturing his ankles. This impact slowed him down so that when he fell onto the pile of tools he only broke 3 vertebrae. As he lay on the tools, in great pain, he finally let go of the rope, causing the empty barrel to fall on him from 80 feet. He survived.

HIGH RISE BOOBS

ENORMOUS BOOBS

An electricity workman broke the basic safety rules when he needed to pee but didn't want to climb down to ground level or even back to the pylon. He was working on the cable itself, which is harmless provided you don't make contact with the ground. This is why birds don't get electrocuted when they sit on electricity cables. But this man decided to open his flies and take a leak from where he was. The stream of urine made an earth contact with the ground and he was fried.

Job Boobs

ENORMOUS BOOBS

A company tried to continue its five-year perfect safety record by showing its workers a film aimed at encouraging the use of safety goggles on the job. Unfortunately, the film's depiction of gory industrial accidents was so graphic that twenty-five workers suffered minor injuries in their rush to leave the screening room. Thirteen others fainted, and one man required seven stitches after he cut his head falling off a chair while watching the film.

A business consultant in Sweden worked for 13 years on a book about the Swedish economy. For safety, he took the 250 page manuscript to be copied. A worker confused the photocopier with the shredder, however, and reduced the manuscript to thousands of tiny strips of paper.

ENORMOUS BOOBS

A Canadian police officer was killed by a fellow officer when he carried out a practical joke at the firing range. He had waited around a corner in the locker room and jumped out to frighten his colleague. The joke worked in that respect . . . his colleague was so shocked that he pulled his gun and shot him in the chest.

An American police officer was demonstrating to his colleagues why it is dangerous to holster a gun with your finger on the trigger. As he did so, the gun fired into an artery in his leg, and he bled to death. Two nights later, another officer was demonstrating how his colleague had shot himself, and he shot himself, too. He tried to drive himself to the hospital, but passed out from blood loss and was killed in the subsequent crash.

Short-sighted Boobs

In 1875, the Director of the United States Patent Office resigned, and recommended that the entire patent office be closed down. His reason for doing so was his belief that there was nothing left to be invented.

Just one year later, in Britain, the Post Office rejected the concept of the telephone on the grounds that most people had access to small boys who could deliver messages for them.

ENORMOUS BOOBS

A nineteenth century blunder ensured that when British soldiers in Africa broke open the ammunition boxes to defend themselves against attacking tribesmen, all they could find inside were biscuits.

When the young Paul McCartney tried to join his local cathedral choir, he was turned down on the basis that he was 'tone deaf and couldn't sing'.

John Lennon's Aunt Mimi used to get fed up with his incessant guitar playing in his bedroom. 'The guitar's all very well,' she told him, 'but you'll never make a living from it.' When John later became a millionaire from his music, he had her words carved on a plaque for her.

SHORT-SIGHTED BOOBS

ENORMOUS BOOBS

Early computers had limited resources, and one way of economising on these resources was to record the year as a two digit number instead of four. This has turned out to be an enormous boob on the part of the designers: with this system, 1972 becomes 72, and the year 2000 becomes 00. It seemed so far away at the time that no one cared. But the implications of a computer thinking that it is the year 00 are enormous: it will assume that it is the year 1900 instead of 2000, which means that it won't chase invoices for 100 years, or it won't continue operating a hospital life support machine, or it will try to wait a century before completing a task it was asked to do the day before.

Mixed Boobs

ENORMOUS BOOBS

The American public boobed in 1938 when they believed a radio dramatisation of H.G. Well's *The War of the Worlds* was a series of genuine reports on the invasion of the earth by Martians.

When a school developed a problem with its older girls pressing their lips against the mirrors in the toilets and leaving prints, the head teacher brought all the girls who wore lipstick into the toilets to meet the caretaker whose job it was to clean it up. The idea was to show them just how difficult it was to clean. The caretaker picked up a long brush and then dipped it in the nearest toilet. Next, he moved to the mirror and proceeded to remove the lipstick. That was the last day the girls pressed their lips on the mirror.

ENORMOUS BOOBS

A French fashion model lost her career because she mistook her husband's hair restorer for breast cream and started growing hair. Great wads of hair began to sprout on her breasts shortly after she accidentally started using the hair-growing cream purchased by her bald-headed husband.

Insurance
Boobs

The following are genuine quotes from motor insurance claim forms:

"I collided with a stationary truck coming the other way."

"A pedestrian hit me and went under my car."

The guy was all over the road. I had to swerve a number of times before I hit him.

I had been driving my car for forty years when I fell asleep at the wheel and had an accident.

INSURANCE BOOBS

ENORMOUS BOOBS

> To avoid hitting the car in front I struck the pedestrian.

> My car was legally parked as it backed into another vehicle.

> An invisible car came out of nowhere, struck my car, then vanished.

> The pedestrian had no idea which direction to go, so I ran over him.

INSURANCE BOOBS

ENORMOUS BOOBS

> I saw the slow-moving, sad-faced old gentleman as he bounced off the roof of my car.

> The telephone pole was approaching fast. I was attempting to move out of its path when it struck my front.

Headline
Boobs

The following are all taken from genuine newspaper headlines:

ENORMOUS BOOBS

SOMETHING WENT WRONG IN JET CRASH, EXPERT SAYS

THE DAILY BOOB

SAFETY EXPERTS SAY SCHOOL BUS PASSENGERS SHOULD BE BELTED

HEADLINE BOOBS

ENORMOUS BOOBS

SURVIVOR OF SIAMESE TWINS JOINS PARENTS

THE DAILY BOOB

PROSTITUTES APPEAL TO POPE

HEADLINE BOOBS

ENORMOUS BOOBS

PANDA MATING FAILS; VET TAKES OVER

THE DAILY BOOB

PLANE
TOO CLOSE TO
GROUND,
CRASH
PROBE
TOLD

HEADLINE BOOBS

ENORMOUS BOOBS

MINERS REFUSE TO WORK AFTER DEATH

JUVENILE COURT TO TRY SHOOTING DEFENDANT

HEADLINE BOOBS

ENORMOUS BOOBS

TWO SOVIET SHIPS COLLIDE, ONE DIES

KILLER SENTENCED TO DIE FOR SECOND TIME IN 10 YEARS

HEADLINE BOOBS

ENORMOUS BOOBS

WAR DIMS HOPE FOR PEACE

THE DAILY BOOB

IF STRIKE ISN'T SETTLED QUICKLY, IT MAY LAST A WHILE

HEADLINE BOOBS

ENORMOUS BOOBS

COLD

WAVE

LINKED TO

TEMPERATURES

THE DAILY BOOB

RED TAPE HOLDS UP NEW BRIDGE

ENORMOUS BOOBS

TYPHOON RIPS THROUGH CEMETERY; HUNDREDS DEAD

MAN
STRUCK BY
LIGHTNING
FACES
BATTERY
CHARGE

HEADLINE BOOBS

153

ENORMOUS BOOBS

THE DAILY BOOB

ASTRONAUT TAKES BLAME FOR GAS IN SPACECRAFT

KIDS MAKE NUTRITIOUS SNACKS

HEADLINE BOOBS

ENORMOUS BOOBS

CHEF THROWS HIS HEART INTO HELPING FEED NEEDY

THE DAILY BOOB

LOCAL HIGH SCHOOL DROPOUTS CUT IN HALF

HEADLINE BOOBS

MAN MINUS EAR WAIVES HEARING

THE DAILY BOOB

SEX
EDUCATION DELAYED, TEACHERS REQUEST TRAINING

HEADLINE BOOBS

Other Humour Books from Summersdale

How To Chat-up Women (Pocket edition)	£3.99
How To Chat-up Men (Pocket edition)	£3.99
Kama Sutra For One *The Single Man's Guide to Self-Satisfaction*	£2.99
101 Uses for a Losing Lottery Ticket	£3.99
Men! Can't Live with them, Can't live *with* them	£3.99
www.wit@wisdom	£4.99
Drinking Games	£3.99
Girl Power	£3.99
Ultimate Chat-up Lines	£3.99
101 Reasons Not To Do Anything *A Collection of Cynical & Defeatist Quotations*	£3.99
A Little Bathroom Book	£3.99
101 Reasons why it's Great to be a Woman	£3.99

Available from all good bookshops or via our website:

www.summersdale.com